HOW DO THEY DO IT?

A
Collection of Wordplays
Revealing
the Sexual Proclivities
of Man and Beast

Edited
by
Reinhold Aman

ISSN 0363-9037
ISBN 0-916500-09-8

First Edition

MALEDICTA PRESS
331 South Greenfield Avenue
Waukesha, Wisconsin 53186

Printed in the United States of America

INTRODUCTION

As indicated in our earlier collection of *do it*'s in *Maledicta*
4, we are presenting stereotyped associations and concepts
of occupations, ethnic groups, religions, individuals,
animals, and the like, by portraying how they allegedly *do it*.

Doing this booklet of *do it*'s seemed so easy: just collect
the entries, alphabetize them, typeset them, and send them
off to the printers. However, your cerebral and seminal
outpourings changed the envisaged 16-page pamphlet in-
to a respectable publication. After nine months of labor
it emerged from the computer's belly, byte by byte. The
projected weekend job had turned into a major book pro-
duction by the time the more than 2,000 *do it*'s were readied
for computerized typesetting by alphabetizing them,
eliminating duplicates, rewriting about 150 contributions,
and coding them for phototypesetting. And I got hooked
again, doing multiple insertions as they popped into my
mind. Now I just have to stop doing it, to get the material
finally into the computer, out to the printer, into the mail,
out to you, and into your hands. It was great fun doing
it. I chuckled a lot.

There are numerous extremely clever contributions from
our Maledicta members and from friendly Mensans. A fair
number (mine included) are obvious or just Sceaux-Sceaux,
as some French wit might be wont to say, but most of them
are very intelligent wordplays of many different kinds. In

a way, *do it*'s are like crossword puzzles, some with obvious clues and others demanding thinking or specialized knowledge. The *ahá*-reaction occurs when you realize the relationship between the two parts (profession and adverb). Some require reading aloud or checking for multiple meanings in a good dictionary to understand them; others drawn from contemporary American culture — advertising included — probably will remain mysterious to non-natives. The wordplays provide a great corpus for linguistic analysis and dissection, but I don't feel like doing it. You do it. Or let George do it.

The *do it*'s are from three sources: from our Maledicta members, from members of Mensa, 225 new ones from me, and my original 163 published in *Maledicta* 4 (1980:174-179). My own 388 *do it*'s are indicated by asterisks.

I wish to thank all Maledicta Society members who did it by sending in from one to more than 150 *do it*'s. Those members marked with an asterisk submitted from 10 to over 150: *Christine Anderson, Mac Barrick, Richard Bean, Sandy Berman, James Burns, Agnes Campbell, *Fred Chambers, *Karen Coogan, *Norman and Margaret Cubberly, Eden Emerson, *Darryl Francis, *Len Frazier, Hans Frommer, *Louise Halperin, *John Henrick (who did it more than grossly, submitting over 144 *do it*'s), Francine Hughes, Michel Janicot, *John Keirstead, Stanford Luce, Wilfrid Malone, Mary "No Name, Please" and hubby, *Douglas McKay, Louisa Otis, Robert Di Pietro, Olaf Prufer, Don Rickter, Bruce Rodgers, *Robert Ryan, *Joseph Salemi, *Karin Steinhaus, *William Tangney, *Robert Throckmorton,*David Anders Tilden,*Leif Tilden, John Valleau, Roy West, and Alma Williams.

Likewise, my thanks are extended to the following Mensa members who did it to Marvin and me by sending in their *do it*'s, responding to Mr. Grosswirth's article on Aman's "Louisianans Do It Bayoutifully" in the *Mensa Bulletin* (July-August 1981). Mensans who submitted over 20 *do it*'s are also honored with a star: Tom Adams, Sharon Akin, *Rita Alcorn, George Appleton, *Charles Bateman, Louis Baumwoll, E.C. Behrman, Joe Bouchard, George Burtt, Mary Byers, *Jay Dunner, Bob Ferris, *Warren and Maureen Fogard, *Sherrill Foote, B.S. Fujimoto, Herman Gelband, Dave Gonzales, Suzanna Goodyear, *Paul Gregg, *Marvin Grosswirth, Daniel Hanley, Sunn Hayward, Anne Hinds, Beth Holler, Bill Jarvis, Carol King, Barry Leff, *Gordon Marhoefer (who graciously permitted use of his copyrighted *do it*'s), Scott McKee, Dorothy Meredith, Burton Meserve, Judith Myers, *G.E. Nordell, *Pat Piper, *Sandra Rimany, Ken Robinson, Dan Romanchik, Audrey Rundquist, Arthur Sabin, Dick Scarritt, Mary Scharadin, Mike Shapiro, Ellen Shelton, Patrick Shepard, Jack Smith, *Sheila Taylor, *John Vancini, Joseph Vles, and Robert Weiner.

To all who have contributed: a big THANK YOU! for doing it.

If we have stimulated you to think up new *do it*'s, please send them to the address below for an expanded edition of this booklet. Like limericks and other verbal goodies, these *do it*'s should be enjoyed in small doses. Don't over-do it!

Reinhold Aman
Maledicta Press
331 S. Greenfield Ave.
Waukesha, Wis. 53186

HOW DO THEY DO IT?

A

Aardvarks do it with their nose.
Abecedarians do it literally.
Abélard and Héloïse did it to their undoing.
Absentminded folks forget where they did it.
Académiciens do it with French letters.
Accountants do it by the numbers.
Accountants do it calculatingly.
Accountants do it in the red.
Accountants do it with their fingers.
Achilles did it with his heel.*
Acrobats do it with a flip.
Actors do it for an encore.
Actors do it for applause.
Actors do it methodically.
Actors do it on cue.
Actors do it in part.
Acupuncturists do it needily.
Ad men do it with multiple insertions.
Adam did it in the evening.
Adam did it with his rib.*
Adam Smith did it with an invisible hand.
Admirals do it fleetingly.*
Adolescents do it in their jeans.
Adolph's does it tenderly.
Adventists do it until the second coming.
Advertisers do it with their house organs.
Aerobatic pilots do it upside down.

Aerospace engineers do it in the air.*
Agronomists do it in the dirt.
Air-condition repairmen do it with cool.
Air traffic controllers do it strikingly, if at all.
Airline clerks do it reservedly.
Airplane stuntmen do it on the wing.
Alexander Graham Bell did it auricularly.
Alexander Graham Bell did it with poles.
Alfred did it great.
Alfred Hitchcock did it horribly.
Alpes-Maritimes dwellers do it Nicely.
Ambitious people do it strivingly.
Amnesiacs don't remember how they did it.
Anesthesiologists do it sleepily.
Anesthesiologists do it unconsciously.*
Anesthetists do it in your sleep.
Anesthetists do it painlessly.
Angostura makers do it bitterly.
Anilinguists do it cheekily.
Anne did it frankly.
Annie Oakley did it with a gun.
Anthropologists do it primitively.*
Anthropologists do it with skeletons.
Anthropologists do it with their old bones.
Anthropologists do it with *homo erectus.*
Antique collectors do it for old time's sake.
Antique dealers do it secondhandedly.
Apiarists do it in hives.
Arabs do it with camels, allegedly.*
Arabs do it with oil.
Archeologists really dig doing it.
Archeologists dig it.
Archeologists do it in the dirt.
Archeologists do it in ruins.
Archeologists do it from underneath.

Archeologists do it in digs.
Archeologists do it with their mummies.
Archeologists do it with their pieces.
Archers do it with a quiver.
Architects do it with a plan.
Aristocrats do it with class.
Aristotle did it meanly.
Arkansans do it opportunely.
Armored-car drivers do it on the brink.
Arsonists do it heatedly.*
Art teachers do it on canvas.
Arthur did it on a round table.
Artillerymen do it with bores of the highest caliber.
Artisans do it craftily.*
Ascetics do it fastidiously.
Asphalters do it in the road.
Astronauts get spaced out doing it.
Astronauts do it by getting their rockets off.
Astronauts do it in free fall.
Astronauts do it spacily.
Astronomers do it at night.
Astronomers do it in clusters.
Astronomers do it in the dark.
Astronomers do it nightly.
Astronomers do it with heavenly bodies.*
Astronomers do it starry-eyed.*
Atheists do it ungodly.*
Athletes do it broadjumpingly.*
Athletes do it dashingly.
Athletes do it on the move.
Athletes do it racily.
Attila did it with his honey.
Attorneys do it appealingly.
Attorneys do it briefly.
Attorneys do it for a fee.

Attorneys do it willingly.
Auctioneers do it unbidden.
Australians do it down under.*
Authors do it write.
Auto racers do it in laps.
Auto workers do it mechanically.
Avis employees try to do it harder.
Ayatollahs don't do it.

B

Bach did it contrapuntally.
Bach did it massively.
Bach did it passionately.
Bacteriologists do it virulently.
Bad check writers do it fraudulently.
Bad river-pilots do it off course.*
Bags do it gladly.
Bakers get a rise out of doing it.
Bakers knead to do it.
Bakers do it after rising.
Bakers do it at 400 degrees.
Bakers do it crumbly.
Bakers do it thirteen times.*
Bakers do it to get bread.
Bakers do it whenever they knead.
Bakers do it with their dough.
Bakers dough it.*
Bald men do it inhairently.*
Ballerinas do it on their toes.
Ballerinas do it with their toes.
Balzac did it with *romans* and *contes*.
Bandleaders do it in step.
Bank clerks do it tellingly.

Bankers do it for money.
Bankers do it interestingly.*
Bankers do it only with collateral.
Bankers do it with interest.
Baptists do it rigidly.
Barbara Walters does it, reportedly.
Barbers do it clippingly.
Barbers do it hairily.
Bargain hunters do it in basements.*
Bargain hunters do it thriftily.
Barmaids do it with their jiggers.
Bartenders do it on the rocks.
Bartenders do it straight up.
Baseball pitchers do it on the mound.
Baseball players do it when they get to third base.
Baseball players do it foully.
Basil does it sagely.
Basketball players do it dribblingly.
Basketball players do it to score.
Bass players do it by plucking around.
Bass players do it standing up.
Bassoonists do it with a *fagott*.
Bathers do it with zest.
Bats do it blindly.
Beadmakers do it all strung out.
Beavers do it busily.*
Beavers do it eagerly.
Beavers do it with their broad, flat tails.*
Beavers do it with their teeth.
Beekeepers do it stingily.
Beekeepers do it veeeeery carefully.
Beekeepers do it with their honey.
Beekeepers get hives when they do it.*
Beer drinkers do it to get ahead.
Beer drinkers do it with gusto.

Bees do it buzzingly.
Bees do it with a buzz.
Beethoven did-did-did-dah'd it.*
Beethoven did it eroically.
Beethoven did it nine times.*
Beginners do it startingly.*
Behaviorists are conditioned to do it.
Belgians do it bilingually.*
Bellhops do it gratuitously.
Ben does it gaily.*
Benefactors do it magnanimously.
Bermudans do it in their shorts.*
Berry growers do it in a jam.
Betty Friedan does it liberally.
Beverly does it on window sills.
Bibliophiles do it voluminously.
Bigots do it intolerably.*
Bigots do it with discrimination.
Bikers do it in the dirt.
Billiard players do it with scattered balls.
Billie Jean King does it lickety-split.
Billy Graham does it on TV.
Billy Graham does it with outstretched arms.*
Biologists do it with animals.*
Bird watchers do it for a lark.
Birds do it early.
Birds do it with exaltation.
Birds do it. Bees do it.
Bishops do it annointedly.
Bishops do it archly.
Bishops do it mitrely.
Blacks do it guardedly.*
Blacks do it kinky.*
Blacks did it slavishly.
Blacksmiths do it by forging on.

Blacksmiths do it to the anvil chorus.
Blacksmiths do it with their hammer.*
Blind people do it touchingly.
Bo did it diddly.
Boars do it whole-hog.*
Boatmen do it volgaly.
Bob does it hopefully.*
Bob Hope does it just as a joke.
Bogart did it as time went by.
Book publishers do it randomly.
Bookkeepers do it with double entries.
Bookkeepers ledger do it.
Bookmakers do it oddly.*
Boris did it godunov.*
Bosses do it firmly.
Bostonians do it properly.
Bottle makers do it without deposit or return.
Bowlers do it in alleys and gutters.
Bowlers do it sparingly.*
Bowlers do it strikingly.
Boxers do it everlastingly.
Boxers do it in their shorts.
Boxers do it matchlessly.
Boxers do it shortly.
Boxers do it until they are punchdrunk.
Boxers do it with their fists.
Brassière manufacturers do it upliftingly.
Brewers do it frothingly.*
Brewers do it hoppily.
Brewers do it in hops.
Bricklayers do it by hand.
Bridge builders do it beamingly.
Bridge players do it in fours.
Bridge players do it with finesse.
Bridge players do it with a slam.

Brooke Shields does it with Calvin.
Brucie does it in Ernest.*
Bruckner did it with his organ.*
Buccaneers frigate.*
Buckminster did it fully.
Bucks doe it.*
Buddha did it sitting down.
Buggers do it retroactively.*
Builders do it by driving in their nails.
Builders do it constructively.
Builders do it until it's erect.
Building workers do it erectly.
Bulls do it hornily.
Bulova watch makers did it once upon a time.
Bulova watch owners do it to unwind.
Burglars do it alarmingly.
Burglars do it with alarm.
Butchers do it by beating their meat.*
Butchers do it choppily.
Butlers do it.

C

Cab drivers do it by the mile.
Cabinet makers do it in their drawers.
Cadavers do it stiffly.
Cads do it leerily.
Cain did it ably.
Calculators do it digitally.
Calendar makers do it daily.
Californians do it laid back.*
Californians do it on shaky grounds.*
Californians do it sharingly.*
Californians do it to a fault.

Calligraphers do it beautifully with their hand.
Calligraphers do it cursively.
Calligraphers do it with a flourish.
Camels do it it humpingly.*
Cameramen do it candidly.
Cameramen do it with dollies.
Campers do it intensely.
Canadian whiskey drinkers do it wryly.
Candle makers do it wickedly.
Cannibals do it less and less.
Cannoneers do it ballistically.*
Canoeists do it with their paddle.*
Captain Queeg did it with steel balls.
Captain did it marvelously.
Car strippers do it tirelessly.
Cardiologists do it heartily.*
Cardiologists do it with heart.
Carl Sagan does it billions and billions of times.
Carnival workers do it fairly.
Carpenters do it handily.
Carpenters do it in their drawers.
Carpenters do it on the level.
Carpenters do it with aplomb.
Carpenters do it with studs.
Carpenters do it with their joints.
Carpenters do it with tongue in groove.
Carpenters do it woodenly.
Carpet layers do it on the floor.
Carpet layers do it on their knees.
Carpet layers do it tackily.
Carroll did it lewisly.
Carter, Sadat and Begin did it summitaneously.
Carter did it plainly.
Carter did it with a jimmy.*
Cashiers do it for a change.

Cashiers do it tellingly.*
Castrati do it on the high C's.
Cat owners do it pusillanimously.
Catfish do it wholly.
Catherine did it great.*
Catholics do it faithfully.
Catholics do it rhythmically.*
Cattle ranchers do it for high steaks.
Cattlemen do it behoovingly.
Cavalrymen did it mulishly.
Cave dwellers do it on the rocks.
CBers do it over and over and over and out.
Cellists do it basely.
Cerberus did it guardedly.
Certified accountants do it publicly.
Cervantes did it quixotically.
Chaingang prisoners do it on the links.
Chameleons do it changeably.
Charlie does it angelically.
Charon did it on styx.*
Chaucer did it one tale after another.
Cheerleaders do it screamingly.*
Cheese makers do it kraftily.
Chefs do it saucily.
Chefs do it spicily.
Chefs do it tastefully.
Chefs do it three times a day.
Chemists do it assiduously.*
Chemists do it organically.
Chemists do it periodically.
Chemists do it sinthetically.
Chemists precipitate doing it.
Cherries do it tartly.
Chess players do it knightly.
Chess players do it *en passant*.

Chicagoans do it it breezily.*
Chinese do it communally.
Chinese do it inscrutably.*
Chinese cooks do it gingerly.
Chinese violin students do it sternly.
Chinese waiters do it wantonly.
Chiquita does it with bananas.
Choral singers do it with glee.
Chorus lines do it in unison.
Christian Scientists monitor it.*
Christians do it guiltily.
Christians do it with gentility.
Church organists do it piously.*
CIA eavesdroppers do it buggingly.
Circe did it with swine.*
Circuitous sodomites do it indreckly.*
Circumcisers do it for a small tip.*
Circus performers do it intently.*
City slickers do it urbanely.*
Claims adjusters do it by accident.
Clams do it all steamed up.
Cleaners do it dryly.
Clementine did it darlingly.
Cleopatra did it snakishly.
Cleopatra did it with her asp.*
Clerics do it religiously.*
Clerics do it soulfully.
Cleavage lovers do it to keep abreast.
Clock-watchers do it with both hands.
Clockmakers do it handily.
Clockmakers do it secondhand.
Clockmakers do it time after time.
Clockmakers do it watchfully.*
Clockmakers do it punctually.*
Clothiers do it wearily.

Clowns do it for a laugh.
Clowns do it funnier.
Clowns do it in jest but make up for it.
Clowns do it strictly for laughs.
Clubmen do it gleefully.
Co-pilots do it without control.
Cobblers do it last.
Cobblers do it to last.
Cockney johns do it with an oar.*
Cods do it for the halibut.
Coffee growers think it's a grind to do it.
Coffee growers do it on the grounds.
College presidents do it by degrees.
Coloradans do it centennially.
Columnists do it against a deadline.
Columnists do it by the inch.
Columnists do it regularly.*
Comedians do it funnily.
Comedians do it standing up.
Comedians do it with their funny bone.
Commercial artists do it graphically.
Commodities traders do it by straddling.
Communists do it collectively.
Communists do it only on their left side.
Complainers do it querulously.
Composers do it with their staff.
Compulsives do it and do it and do it again.
Compulsives do it neatly.*
Computer operators do it bit by bit.*
Computer operators do it with peripherals.
Computer operators do it with drives and mounts.
Computer programmers do it with bytes.
Concert pianists do it grand.
Conductors do it by waving their batons.
Conductors do it with their baton.

Confectioners do it sweetly.*
Confectioners do it with malted balls.
Connecticutters do it constitutionally.
Conservatives do it right.
Conservatives do it with restraint.
Convicts do it penally.
Convicts do it while begging your pardon.
Cookie bakers do it gingerly.
Cooks do it choppily.
Cooks do it stirringly.
Coprophiles do it interred.*
Coprophiles do it shittily.*
Cops do it friskily.
Corn growers do it with their ears.
Cornishmen do it with hens.*
Coroners get stiff when they do it.
Coroners do it stiffly.
Corporals do it privately.
Correspondents do it with a stamped,
self-addressed envelope.
Cottage owners do it cheesily.
Counterfeiters do it fakingly.
Court reporters do it on a trial basis.
Cowards do it with their yellow bellies.*
Cowboys do it bareback.
Cowboys do it in the saddle.
Cowboys do it on horseback.
Cowboys do it saddly.
Cowboys do it with their boots on.
Cowgirls do it in stirrups.
Crane operators do it upliftingly.*
Cricketeers do it wickedly.
Crocodiles do it tearfully.*
Crossword fans do it going down and coming across.
Crows do it scarily.*

Crustaceans do it crabbily.*
Cubans do it with fidelity.
Cunnilinguists do it succinctly.*
Curators do it collectively.
Customs inspectors do it dutifully.*
Customs officials do it tariffically.*
Cutlery makers fork it.*
Cyclotron operators do it smashingly.
Cymbalists do it resoundingly.
Cynics do it doggedly.*

D

Da Vinci did it inventively.
Dancers do it with their feet.
Darwin did it originally.
Data processors are programmed to do it.
Date growers do it with their palms.
David does it brinkly.
Deans do it dizzily.*
Debaters do it orally.
Deer hunters do it for a buck.
Defendants do it allegedly.
Defenestrators do it through a window.
Defense attorneys do it objectingly.*
Del Monte does it cannily.
Delinquent debtors do it in arrears.
Democrats do it liberally.
Demolition workers do it explosively.
Demons do it possessively.
Dentists do it down in the mouth.
Dentists do it fillingly.
Dentists do it in cavities.*
Dentists do it in your mouth.*

Dentists do it inextricably.*
Dentists do it painfully.*
Dentists do it painlessly.
Dentists do it with novocaine.
Dentists do it with their drills.
Dentists do it with their tool in your mouth.
Dentists do it with your gums.*
Dentists pull it.*
Denverites do it higher.
Dermatologists do it flakily.*
Descartes thought he did it, therefore he did it.
Desdemona did it breathlessly.
Detectives do it under cover.
Devil worshippers do it for the hell of it.
Diamond experts do it brilliantly.
Diarists do it chronically.
Dickens did it with great expectations.
Dickie Cavett does it very self-consciously.*
Digital designers do it logically.
Dilettantes do it superficially.
Dinghy sailors do it between the sheets.
Diplomats do it tactfully.
Distillers do it wryly.
Divers do it deeper.
Divers do it head first.
Divers do it muffedly.*
Divers do it swimmingly.
Divers do it without coming up for air.
Dobermans do it pinchingly.
Doctors do it indecipherably.
Doctors do it with patience.
Doctors do it with practice.
Dog lovers do it with grooming.
Dogs do it cynically.*
Dolphins do it flippantly.*

21

Dolphins do it on porpoise.
Don Rickles does it with his vicious mouth.*
Donkeys do it asininely.
Donne did it metaphysically.
Donors do it givingly.
Doormen do it openly.
Doris does it daily.
Dr. Frankenstein did it igorly.
Draftsmen do it leadenly.
Draftsmen do it sketchily.
Draftsmen do it with a pencil.
Drama critics do it with new openings.
Dramatists do it in three acts.
Drapery hangers do it with long rods.
Dressmakers do it on pins and needles.
Dressmakers do it fittingly.
Dressmakers do it seamingly.
Drill operators do it boringly.*
Drill sergeants do it by the numbers.
Drill sergeants do it double-time.
Drill teams do it with precision.
Drinkers do it spiritually.*
Drummers do it by beating it.
Drummers do it differently.*
Drummers do it with a bang.
Drunks do it groggily.*
Drunks do it rollingly.
Duck hunters do it blindly.
Ducks do it with a quack.
Duns Scotus did it subtly.
Dustmen do it dirtily.
Dutch lesbians do it with their dikes.
Dwarfs do it shortly.*
Dyslectics od ti.

E

E. Power Biggs did it with his organ.
Eagles do it high up.
Ecdysiasts undo it.
Ecdysiasts do it with a shake.
Economists do it by supply and demand.
Economists do it efficiently.
Ed McMahon guffaws indiscriminately
whenever Johnny Carson does it.*
Edgar Allan Poe did it ravenously.
Edgar Allan did it poely.*
Edison did it electronically.
Edison did it patently.
Editors do it grumpily.*
Editors do it with blue pencils.
Egyptian mummies do it windingly.
Egyptologists do it with their mummies.
Einstein did it relatively.*
El Salvadorans do it revoltingly.
Electrical engineers do it until it Hz.
Electricians do it amply.
Electricians do it lightly.
Electricians do it shockingly.
Electricians do it revoltingly.
Electricians do it with a jolt.
Electronics engineers do it unbiasedly.*
Elephants do it with their trunk.*
Elizabeth Taylor does it stoutly.
Elmer does it stickily.
Elvis did it with his pelvis.*
Emma Bovary did it with venom.
Emperors do it majestically.*
Employers like to withhold it.
Endocrine glands do it secretively.

Engineers do it mechanically.*
Engineers do it to spec.
Engineers do it with precision.
Engineers do it with slow strokes.
English teachers do it with dangling participles.
Englishmen do it politely.
Englishmen do it with a stiff upper lip.
Entomologists do it on the fly.
Enuretics do it on a rubber mat.
Epictetus did it stoically.
Epidemiologists do it contagiously.
Epileptics do it fitfully.
Equestrians do it hoarsely.
Equestrians do it whoafully.
Equestrians do it with horses.*
Eric did it redily.
Ernest and Julio Gallo do it in bottles.
Errant spouses do it with abandon.
Eschatologists do it heavenly or hellishly.
Eskimos do it coldly.*
est graduates do it for the experience.
Etchers do it bitingly.
Etymologists do it with their roots and stems.*
Euclid did it geometrically.
Eunuchs do it uniquely.*
Eunuchs do it with no hard feelings.
Eunuchs would do it if they had balls.
Europeans do it by the meter, Americans by the inch.
Eve did it adamantly.
Ex-National Guardsmen do it without reserve.
Exhibitionists do it flashily.*
Exhibitionists do it in a flash.
Existentialists do it absurdly.
Experts do it authoritatively.*
Experts do it unfailingly.

F

Fair-weather friends do it in April, May and June.
Fanatics do it rigidly.
Fanny Farmer does it sweetly.
Farmers do it at the crack of dawn.*
Farmers do it to plant their seeds.
Fatalists do it inevitably.
Faust did it devilishly.
Felines do it cattily.*
Fellators do it headily.
Female impersonators drag it out.
Fencers do it pointedly.
Fertile women do it periodically.
Fiddle players do it without fretting.
Field marshals do it strategically.*
Film directors do it on their flatbeds.
Film editors do it with white gloves.
Film makers do it with interlock.
Finns do it fishy.*
Finns do it steamingly.
Fire-eaters make an ash of themselves when they do it.
Firefighters do it hotly.*
Firemen do it alarmingly.
Firemen do it heatedly.*
Firemen do it with their hoses.
Firemen do it with their hoses stiff.
Fish do it in schools.
Fishermen do it luringly.
Fishermen do it with baited breath.
Fishermen do it with their rods.
Fishwives do it sellfishly.*
Flashers do it openly.
Fliers do it on autopilot.
Flight instructors teach you how to do it
when you're up.

Floor sanders do it with true grit.
Florists do it with tulips.
Flutists do it for trills.*
Fly-casters do it with longer rods.
Folklorists do it orally.
Football players do it quarterly.
Former fellatrixes 8 it.*
Fortune tellers do it with crystal balls.*
Founders do it dumbly.
Fox hunters do it lairily.
Foxes do it cunningly.
Frank Lloyd Wright did it with an erection.
Frank Lloyd did it Wright.
Frank Sinatra doobie-doobie-does it.
Frankenstein did it monstrously.*
Franklin did it inventively.
Fred Astaire does it gingerly.
French chefs do it saucily.
Frenchmen do it frankly.*
Freud did it in his sleep.
Frogmen do it squatted.
Frugal skunks do it cent by cent.
Fruit packers do it cannily.
Funeral bands do it in Key Largo.
Furniture makers do it chairily.

G

G. Bernard Shaw did it with pig, ma, lion.*
Galileo did it with heavenly spheres.*
Gamblers do it in hedges.
Gamblers do it oddly.
Ganders do it with a goose.
Garbage collectors do it cannily.

Garbagemen do it collectively.
Gardeners do it in the dirt.
Gardeners do it potted.
Gargoyles do it grotesquely.
Garnish growers do it sparsely.
Gasoline-siphoners do it with a sucking action.
Gastroenterologists do it with guts.
Gate-keepers do it swingingly.
Gay rabbis do it with their shofar.*
Gays do it queerly.
Gene does it inherently.
Genealogists do it in a family way.
Genghis Khan do it.
Geniuses do it until it smarts.
Geoducks do it clammily.
Geologists do it prospectively.
Geologists do it with their rocks.
Geometers do it by erecting a perpendicular.
Geometricians do it plainly.
Georgians do it peachy.*
Georgie did it porgily.
Gerald does it in a ford.
Germans do it in a sourly crowd.*
Germans do it markedly.*
Germans do it when ordered to.
Germans do it wurst.
Gershwin did it rhapsodically.*
Ghosts do it ghastly.*
Ghosts do it spookily.
Gibbons do it swingingly.*
Gigolos do it when they're hard up.
Gillespie does it dizzily.*
Girls do it manfully.
Glaziers do it panefully.
Glider pilots do it quietly.

Glossologists do it with divers tongues.
God did it creatively.
Godzilla did it frightfully.*
Goldsmiths do it with a lot of gilt.
Golfers do it until it's in the hole.
Golfers do it 18 times a day.
Golfers do it by the stroke.
Golfers do it in the rough.
Golfers do it parfully.
Golfers do it to a tee.
Golfers do it with a handicap.
Golfers do it with a hole in one.
Golfers do it with a stiff shaft.
Golfers do it with as few strokes as possible.
Golfers do it with lots of balls.
Golfers do it with their putters.
Gossips do it, then tell everyone about it.*
Gossips do it across the fence.
Gourmets do it delectably.
Gourmets do it tastefully.
Gourmets do it with a mouth-watering dish.*
Gourmets do it with white sauce.
Graduate students do it by degrees.
Gräfenberg did it with the G-spot.*
Graffitists do it on the wall.
Grammarians do it infinitively.
Grammarians do it punctually.*
Gravediggers do it in the dirt.
Greeks do it with tongue in cheek.
Gregory did it enchantingly.*
Grenadiers do it guardedly.
Greyhounds do it busily.
Groupies do it famously.
Guitar players do it sitting down.
Guitarists do it fretfully.

Guitarists do it with a G string.
Gulls do it unherringly.
Gurus do it masterfully.
Gurus do it spiritually.
Gymnasts do it flippantly.
Gynecologists do it at the orifice.
Gynecologists do it cunningly.*
Gynecologists do it with stirrups.
Gypsies do it with crystal balls.

H

H & R Block do it but find it taxing.
Hadassah women do it bazaarly.
Haig does it commandingly.
Hairdressers do it permanently.*
Hairdressers do it with style.
Hairdressers do it teasingly.
Halibut do it flounderingly.
Ham operators do it with varying frequency.
Handel did it with high din.
Handymen do it with a lick and a promise.
Harpsichordists do it pluckily.
Hatters do it madly.
Hawaiians do it isolatedly.*
Head nurses do it on their knees.*
Health dieters do it organically.
Hebrew delicatessen owners do it judiciously.
Hegelians do it synthetically.
Heisenberg did it uncertainly.
Helen Keller did it blindly.
Helen Keller did it unsoundly.
Helen Keller did it with her fingers.
Helen does it reddily.*

Helpless people do it with their hands tied.
Hemotologists do it sanguinarily.
Hemstitchers do it seemingly.
Henry did it thoreauly.*
Henry did it tudorifically.
Hens do it broodingly.
Hens do it cluckingly.
Herb gardeners do it ruefully.
Hermaphrodites do it selfishly.*
Hermits do it alone.
Herpes victims do it but they'll never tell.
Herpetologists do it snakily.
Herr Bayer did it aspiringly.
Herring do it redily.
Heterosexual males do it unassailably.*
Hiawatha did it without reservations.
Hikers do it in their boots.
Himalayans do it mountingly.
Hiram did it walking.
Historians do it chronically.*
Historians did it in the past.
Hitchhikers do it with their thumbs.*
Hitler did it führiously.
Hitters do it pinch by pinch.
Hockey players do it by pucking around.
Hockey players do it puckishly.
Homosexuals do it gaily.
Homosexuals do it half in earnest.
Honored guests do it occasionally.
Hookers do it horribly.
Hookers do it with tricks.
Horologists do it around the clock.
Horselovers do it in the main.
Horticulturists do it peachily.
Hot bun bakers do it crossly.

Hot dog vendors do it with relish.
Hot rodders do it in drag.
Hotel keepers do it sweetly.
Hotheads do it quickly.*
Housewives do it with hamburger helpers.
Howdy did it doodifully.
Huey did it longer.
Hume did it empirically.
Humpty-Dumpty did it off the wall.
Huns did it ravishingly.
Hunters do it when they can find it.
Hyenas do it hysterically.
Hypnotists do it at the snap of a finger.
Hypnotists do it subliminally.

I

Ideologists do it in their mind.
Ignoramuses do it unknowingly.*
Ike and Nehru did it in their jackets.*
Illiterates do it indescribably.*
Imitators do it apishly.
Immanuel Kant did it categorically.
Immigrants used to do it on the old sod.*
Impotent men do it softly.
Incompetent cardio-surgeons do it halfheartedly.*
Indexers do it one by one.
Indian guides do it unerringly.*
Indians do it bravely.
Indians do it chiefly.
Indians do it givingly.
Indians do it to be brave.
Indians do it without reservations.*
Infielders do it basely.

Insomniacs do it restlessly.*
Insomniacs do it with open eyes.*
Insurance men do it as a matter of policy.
Insurgents do it revoltingly.
Intellectuals do it with their head.*
Interior finishers do it plastered.
Inventors do it originally.
Inventors do it patently.
Investors do it in well-balanced portfolios.
Irenics do it peacefully.*
Ironworkers do it ferociously.
Italian bankers do it leerily.
Italian terrorists do it with your kneecap.*
Itzhak Perlman does it with his bow.
Ivan did it terribly.*

J

Jack Horner did it with a plum.
Jack the Ripper did it piece by piece.
Jack did it rippingly.
Jackie Bovine Kennedy did it on asses.*
Jackrabbits do it and do it and do it.
Jacques Cousteau does it under water.*
Jailbirds do it in confinement.
Jakob and Wilhelm did it grimmly.*
James Watt does it with wild abandonment.
Jane Byrne does it merrily.
Janitors flush after they do it.
Janitors do it cleanly.
Janitors do it in a drum.
Japanese do it nippily.
Japanese do it shamefully.
Jedi do it with force.

Jekyll does it experimentally, then hydes.

Jesus Christ did it crossly.

Jewelers do it brilliantly.*

Jill did it tumblingly.

Jim Beam does it cornily.

Jimmy Carter did it with lust in his heart.

Jimmy Carter did not do it for peanuts.*

Jockeys do it briefly.

Jockeys do it hoarsely.

Jockeys do it horsing around.

Jockeys do it in their shorts.

Jockeys do it strappingly.

Jockeys do it stridently.

Jockeys do it supportively.

Jockeys do it with whip and spurs.

Joe Clark does it conservatively.

Joggers do it on the run.

Johann Sebastian did it bachwards.

John Birchers do it extremely right.

John Calvin did it with predetermination.

John Galway does it with his flute.*

John the Baptist did it with his head.

John Wayne did it with his fist.

John Wayne did it with true grit.

Johnny Carson does it four times a week.*

Jokers do it practically.

Jonathan did it swiftly.

Journal publishers do it quarterly.

Journalists do it reportedly.*

Judas did it treacherously.*

Judges do it by the book.

Judges do it in their chambers.

Judges do it judiciously.*

Judges do it on the bench.

Judges do it with conviction.

Jugglers do it with balls and clubs.
Juries do it deliberately.
Justice O'Connor does it supremely well.

K

Kangaroos do it in court.
Kant did it categorically and imperatively.
Kareem Abdul Jabbar does it dunkingly.
Karl Marx did it kapitally.
Keyboardists do it with portable organs.
Kindergartners do it primarily.
King Arthur did it knightly nightly.*
King Arthur did it with his lance a lot.
King Kong did it Fay's way.
Kings do it royally.*
Kite flyers keep it up longer with a piece of tail.
Kite flyers do it with strings attached.
Klansmen do it sheetily.
Klansmen do it under the sheets.
Knights did it chivalrously.
Knights did it boldly.*

L

Lady voyeurs do it cock-eyed.
Lager brewers do it headily.
Land title investigators do it abstractly.
Lassie did it bitchily.
Latin scholars do it supinely.
Laurel did it hardly.*
Lawbreakers do it offensively.*
Lawrence of Arabia did it between humps.

Lawrence Welk does it accordingly.
Lawyers do it appealingly.
Lawyers do it briefly.
Lawyers do it in their briefs.
Lawyers do it on a trial basis.
Lawyers do it with better motions.
Leatherworkers do it with belts and straps.
Lecturers lecher do it.*
Leif did it luckily, and so did Pierre.
Lensmakers do it objectively.*
Leopards do it spottily.
Lesbians do it cliterally.*
Lesbians do it insurmountably.*
Lesbians do it with their bosom buddies.
Lesbians dildo it.*
Levi Strauss does it pantingly.
Lewis Carroll did it, but all he got was bandersnatch.
Lexicographers do it alphabetically.
Lexicographers do it definitively.
Lexicographers do it demeaningly.
Lexicographers do it verbosely.
Liability insurers do it under blanket coverage.
Liars do it fabulously.
Liars do it unbelievably.
Libertines do it freely.*
Librarians deweyt.*
Librarians overdue it.
Librarians do it by the book.
Librarians do it quietly.
Limericists do it pundamentally.
Linda Lovelace did it throatily.
Lindberg did it while his spirit was in St. Louis.
Lingerie salesmen do it in bras and panties.
Linguists do it cunningly.
Linguists do it with their tongues.

Linus Pauling did it with vitamin C.
Lion tamers do it with a whip.
Lion tamers do it with big pussies.*
Lions do it manely for kids.
Lions do it with pride.
Lithographers do it stoned.
Little Bo Peep did it sheepishly.
Little Boy Blue did it with his horn.
Livestock men do it with their fodder.
Lizards do it leapingly.
Lizzie Borden did it parenthetically.
Loansharks do it vigorishly.
Lobsters turn red doing it.
Lobstermen do it with buoys.
Logicians do it propositionally.
Londoners do it foggily.
Londoners do it in a fog.
Lonely shepherds do it sheepishly.
Long John Silver did it limply.
Longshoremen do it on their peers.
Louisianans do it bayoutifully.*
Luther Burbank did it with pansies.
Lutherans do it by faith alone.

M

Magazine publishers do it periodically.
Magellan did it exploringly.
Magicians do it, then disappear.
Magicians do it inexplicably.*
Magicians do it trickily.
Magicians do it with doves and rabbits.*
Magicians do it with mirrors.
Magicians do it with their wands.

Magistrates do it judiciously.

Maids do it while making the bed.

Mailmen do it for you, but you have to lick your own.

Mailmen do it first-class.

Mailmen do it posthaste.

Mailmen do it with a full bag.

Mailmen do it zippingly.*

Mallards do it duckingly.

Malory did it on the round table.

Mandoline players pick away doing it.

Manic-depressives do it both ways.

Manicurists do it handily.

Manicurists do it with polish.

Manson did it helter-skelter.

Manual laborers do it by hand.*

Marathon runners do it longer.*

Marathoners do it on the run.

Margaret Thatcher does it downingly: a perfect ten.

Marines do it on land, sea, and in the air.

Mark Twain did it with his Mammoth Cod.*

Market analysts do it graphically.

Marksmen do it with a bang.

Marlin Perkins did it cagily.

Marlon Brando did it on the waterfront.*

Martin Luther did it protestingly — 95 times!*

Martini drinkers do it dryly.

Mary does it contrary.

Marylanders do it freely.

Masochists do it for a licking.

Masochists do it for kicks.

Masochists do it painstakingly.

Masons do it but keep it secret.

Masons do it stonily.

Masons do it to get stoned.

Masons do it with their bricks.*

Masters do it baitingly.*
Masters and Johnson do it objectively.
Mastiffs do it bully.
Masturbators do it singlehandedly.*
Matadors do it with a lot of bull.
Matchmakers do it strikingly.
Mathematicians do it by the numbers.
Mathematicians do it calculatingly.
Mathematicians do it constantly.
Mathematicians do it figuratively.*
Mathematicians do it with a slide rule.
Mathematicians do it with square roots.
Mathematicians do it with sum.
Mathematicians do it accurately.
Mead tasters do it mellifluously.
Mechanics only torque about it.
Mechanics do it with their tools.*
Mechanics do it wrenchingly.
Megalomaniacs do it really great.*
Mehta and Bernstein do it in concert.*
Melina Mercouri never does it on Sunday.*
Mensans do it cerebrally.*
Mensans do it only in gray matter.
Mensans do it intelligently.
Mensans do it monthly.*
Mensans do it with their heads.
Menstruating women do it cursively.*
Mercator did it with his projection.*
Merkin makers do it in lap land.
Merlin did it magically.
Meteorologists do it stormily.
Mexicans do it jumpily.
Mexicans do it with wet backs.
Michael Foot does it labouriously.
Michelangelo did it on his back.*

Mickey did it mouse-to-mouse.*
Mickey did it mousily.*
Mickey did it on a mantle.
Midgets do it shortly.
Midwesterners do it corny.*
Military men do it for an honorable discharge.*
Milkmaids do it fetchingly.
Millers do it grindingly.
Miners do it with their shaft.*
Miners' wives do it and get shafted.
Miniaturists do it as little as possible.
Ministers do it primely.
Minnesotans gopher it.
Mirror makers do it with reflection.
Misanthropes do it crotchetly.
Missing persons do it with abandon.
Mistress Mary did it contrarily.
Moby did it with his dick.
Modern English teachers do it good,
like he or she should.*
Mollusks do it spinelessly.*
Mona Lisa did it smilingly.
Money market agents do it without penalty
for premature withdrawal.
Monkeys do it swingingly.
Monks do it cowly.
Monks do it orderly.
Monoglots do it unilingually.*
Monopolists do it exclusively.
Montezuma did it revengefully.
Moonshiners do it with their sugar.
Morticians do it as a solemn undertaking.
Morticians do it cryptically.
Morticians do it gravely.
Morticians do it rigorously.

Moses did it with a burning bush.*
Moses did it lawfully.
Moses did it on a mountain.*
Moses did it with tablets.*
Mother and father did it, apparently.
Mothers do it expectantly.
Motorcycle riders do it with full throttle.
Motorcyclists do it in their helmets.
Motorcyclists do it sitting astride.
Motorcyclists do it speedily.
Motorcyclists do it wearing leather.
Motorcyclists do it with chains.
Motorcyclists do it with their boots on.
Motorcyclists do it with their handlebars.
Motorcyclists do it without a spare rubber.
Motorists do it exhaustingly.*
Mount St. Helens does it to get its rocks off.
Mount St. Helens dwellers do it in the ash.*
Mount St. Helens people do it eruptively.
Mountain climbers do it because it's there.
Mountain climbers do it on top.
Mountain climbers do it to get high.
Mountaineers do it condescendingly.*
Mountaineers do it with picks.
Movers do it on their dollies.
Movie stars do it for show.
Mozart did it with his magic flute.*
Muleteers do it with their whip.*
Murphy did it lawfully.
Mushroom growers do it sporatically.
Musicians do it best with pieces they know.
Musicians do it harmonically.*
Musicians do it in concert.
Musicians do it with rhythm.
Mussolini did it with his chin.*

Mussorgsky did it modestly.*
Myopics do it shortsightedly.*

N

Nannies do it in orthopedic shoes.
Napoleon did it and pulled his bone apart.
Napoleon did it with his bony part.
Narcoleptics do it sleepily.*
National Guardsmen do it on weekends.
Natural food fans do it with their honey.
Navigators do it, of course.
Navigators do it when they're coarse.
Navymen do it fleetingly.
Nazis did it with their arms in the air.
NCO's do it with their privates.
Nebraskans do it huskily.
Necrophiles do it immortally.*
Necrophiliacs do it stiffly.
Neurologists do it nervously.
Neurotics do it compulsively.
New Yorkers do it empirically.
Newsmen do it daily.
Newsmen do it in the presses.
Nietzsche did it supermanfully.
Night club comics do it standing up.
Night watchmen do it all night long.
Night watchmen do it for security.
Nijinsky did it madly.
Nitwits do it unwittingly.*
Nixon deep-sixed it.
Nixon did it ten times before he got it down pat.
Nixon did it with resignation.
Noel did it cowardly.

Non-Jews do it gentilely.
North Carolinans do it tardily.
Notaries do it publicly.
Novelists do it with characters.*
Nouveaux riches do it upwardly.*
Nuclear physicists do it radiantly.
Nudists barely do it.
Nudists do it barely.*
Nuns do it habitually.*
Nuns do it on their knees.*
Nuns do it out of habit.
Nuns do it to get rid of their habits.
Nurses do it with care.
Nurses do it with more patience.
Nurses do it with their stethoscope.
Nymphs do it constantly.

O

Oboists do it reedily.
Obsessive-compulsives redo it.
Obstetricians do it prematurely.
Ocarina players do it with their small instruments.*
Occam did it with a razor.
Oceanographers do it currently.
Oedipus did it complexly.
Oedipus did it filially.
Oedipus did it maternally.
Oedipus did it with his mother.*
Officers do it brassily.
Oilmen do it lubriciously.
Oil refinery workers do it crudely.*
Oilworkers do it well.
Oklahomans do it sooner.

Old bruins do it just barely.
Old women do it loosely.*
Oliver Goldsmith did it vicariously.
Oliver did it twistedly.*
Olympians do it on the run.
Omahans do it mutually.*
Opera singers do it for trills.
Opera singers do it with their diaphragm.
Operating engineers do it with heavy equipment.
Ophthalmologists do it detachedly.
Ophthalmologists do it with pupils.
Ophthalmologists do it with their eyes open.
Ophthalmologists do it with the greatest of E's.
Optometrists do it with vision.
Optimists do it hopefully.
Oragenitalists do it 69 ways.
Orange growers do it in the navel.
Orchard owners do it 'appily.
Organized laborers do it strikingly.
Ornithologists do it cockily.
Orthodontists do it bracingly.
Orthopedists do it with bones.
Orthopedists do it with stiff joints.
Orville and Wilbur did it flyingly.
Oscar Mayer does it frankly.
Oscar Wilde did it queerly.*
Oscar did it wildly.
Osteopaths do it with their bones.*
Oswald Spengler declined to do it.
Overweight people do it fatuously.
Owls do it wisely.*
Oxen do it yokingly.
Oystermen do it in beds.

P

Pablo Picasso did it on canvas.
Pagans do it in the woods.
Painters do it *al fresco.*
Painters do it colorfully.*
Painters do it on a ladder.
Painters do it with even strokes.
Painters do it with longer strokes.
Pancake eaters do it surreptitiously.
Panhandlers do it sparely.
Papermakers do it with chains.
Parachutists do it ripped.
Paramecia do it asexually.
Paramedics do it mouth-to-mouth.*
Paranoids do it suspiciously.*
Parasites do it lousy.
Parentless people do it orphan.
Parents don't do it.
Parents used to do it.
Park rangers do it from the Tetons
down to the Grand Canyon.
Parrots do it repetitiously.
Part-timers just do it on the side.
Pastry chefs do it with tarts.
Pastry cooks do it creamily.
Patti does it page by page.
Paul Harvey does it righteously.*
Paul Masson won't do it before it's time.
Paul Volcker does it with reserve.
Paupers do it poorly.
Pavers do it in the street.
Pavlov's dog did it salivatingly.*
Pawn brokers do it with three balls.
Peasants do it villainously.*

Pederasts do it annually; i.e., *per anum.* *
Pederasts do it gaily.
Pediatricians do it kiddingly.
Pediatricians do it with children.
Pedophiles do it childishly.
Peeping toms do it clandestinely.
Penguins do it cooly and formally.
Pennsylvanians do it eerily.
People who have pedicures do it atonally.
People with flat tires do it sparingly.
Percussionists do it by beating it.
Perfectionists do it hair-splittingly.
Perfume testers do it with their noses.
Persians do it furtively.
Pessimists do it depressingly. *
Pessimists do it negatively.
Pessimists don't do it.
Peter Pan does it with fairies.
Peter and Paul did it sanctimoniously. *
Pharmacists do it dopily. *
Pharmacists do it with their pestle.
Pharyngologists do it in your throat. *
PhD's do it by degrees.
Philadelphians do it with their loving brothers. *
Philanthropists keep it in check.
Philanthropists do it generously.
Phillip does it with mares. *
Phillip does it with Morris. *
Philosophers do it questionably. *
Philosophers don't do it, but they think about it a lot.
Phone booth cheats do it sluggishly.
Photographers do it behind shutters.
Photographers do it candidly.
Photographers do it in a dark room.
Photographers do it in the dark.

Photographers do it negatively.
Photographers do it to see what develops.
Photographers do it with exposure.
Photographers do it with a shudder.*
Photographers do it with flash.
Photographers snap it.
Phrenologists do it bumpily.
Physicists do it with force.
Pianists do it flatly.
Pianists do it Handely.
Pianists do it sharply.
Piano tuners do it well-tempered.
Pierre Trudeau does it liberally.
Pigeons do it monumentally.
Pigs do it sloppily.*
Pigs do it snortingly.
Pillow makers get down to it.
Pilots do it higher up.
Pilots do it on the fly.
Pilots do it plainly.
Pilots do it solo.
Pilots do it flightily.
Pinup girls do it figuratively.
Pirates do it on a dead man's chest.
Pistol-shooters do it automatically.
Pitchers with loaded bases do it bawling.
Pitchers do it low and inside.
Pizza chefs do it by throwing their dough around.
Planners do it systematically.
Planters do it punchily.
Plastic surgeons do it to save face.
Plato did it idealistically.
Playwrights do it climactically.
Planck did it constantly.
Plumbers do it even when they're drained.

Plumbers do it fittingly.
Plumbers do it with a snake.
Plumbers do it with ballcocks.
Plumbers do it with their helpers.
Plumbers do it with leaky pipes.
Plumbers do it with steel pipes.
Plumbers do it with their plungers.
Plumbers do it with water.
Plumbers do it without leaks.
Plumbers do it wrenchingly.
Podiatrists do it by the foot.
Poets do it with their feet, or verse.*
Poker players do it with their ante.
Pole vaulters do it on the rise.
Poles do it magnetically.
Poles do it with polish.*
Police officers do it with their nightstick.*
Policemen do it forcefully.
Political prisoners do it in bondage.
Politicians do it graftily.
Pollsters do it randomly.
Poltergeists do it with spirit.
Pool-sharks do it on cue.
Poor typists do it with one finger.
Popes do it bullishly.
Popes do it dogmatically.
Popes do it infallibly.
Popes do it with bulls.*
Porcupines do it very carefully.
Porno film makers do it for reel.
Post-menopause women do it unbearably.*
Postal clerks do it with dispatch.
Postal workers do it for a raise.
Potters do it with a slip.
PR men do it with releases.

Preachers do it prayerfully.
Prestidigitators do it with sleight of hand.
Priests don't do it.
Priests do it crossly.
Priests do it frockingly.
Priests do it in the rectory.
Priests do it massively.
Priests do it vicariously. *
Priests do it when caught by the organ.
Prince Albert did it in a can. *
Prince Albert did it victoriously.
Prince Charles does it regally.
Prince Charles does it royally.
Prince Rainier did it with grace.
Printers do it typically.
Printers do it with devices.
Printers do it with their own type.
Printers do it impressively. *
Printers do it without wrinkling the sheets.
Privates do it corporally.
Probate clerks do it willingly.
Procrastinators never get around to doing it.
Procrastinators do it later. *
Proctologists do it in heaps. *
Proctologists do it rectally.
Professors do it absentmindedly.
Professors do it testily. *
Programmers do it byte by byte.
Programmers do it in the dumps.
Programmers do it on the tube.
Programmers do it sequentially.
Programmers do it with fewer bytes.
Prospectors claim to do it.
Prostitutes do it profitably.
Prostitutes do it tartly. *

Prostitutes do it whorizontally.*
Psychiatrists do it shrinkingly.
Psychiatrists do it on the couch.
Psychics do it in the future.
Psychics do it mindfully.
Psychoanalysts do it with guilt complexes.
Psychologists do it testily.
Public relations people do it for exposure.
Publishers do it by the book.
Punk rockers do it with safety pins.
Puppeteers do it with their hands.
Pyromaniacs do it in the heat of the night.
Pythagoras did it squarely on the hypotenuse.
Pythagoras did it theoretically.

Q

Quails do it in coveys.
Quakers do it friendlier.
Quakers do it piecefully.*
Quarterbacks do it offensively.
Quarterbacks do it passively.
Quartets do it in barber shops.
Queen Elizabeth does it II.*
Queen Elizabeth does it majestically.
Queen Mary did it bloodily.
Queens do it to bee or not to bee.
Queers do it gaily.
Quilters do it piece by piece.

R

Rabbis do it briskly.
Rabbits do it hairily.*
Rabbits do it hoppily.
Rabelais did it pantingly and gruelly.*
Raccoons wash it and then do it.
Racers do it quickly.
Racquetball players do it on the wall.
Radio operators do it signally.
Radiologists do it glowingly.
Radiologists do it x-ratedly.
Railroad engineers do it tenderly.*
Ray Charles does it blindly.
Reagan does it cuttingly.
Realists do it matter-of-factly.
Record producers do it groovy.*
Redheads do it with flair.
Reindeer do it with whips and harness.
René Levesque does it separately.
Reporters do it sensationally.*
Representatives do it in congress, page by page.
Researchers do it probingly.
Revenue agents do it taxingly.
Revenue service employees do it internally.
Rhetoricians do it eloquently.*
Rich girls do it while watching their fiscal periods.
Rich people do it in their shelters.
Rich people do it with holdings.
Richter did it earthshakingly.*
Riveters do it while it's hot.
Robinson Crusoe did it on Friday.
Robots do it mechanically.
Robots do it with i.c.s.
Rock stars do it by bopping their teenies.

Rock stars do it for the record.
Rodent-lovers do it mouth-to-mouse.*
Rogers does it gingerly.*
Roman Polanski does it with childlike enthusiasm.
Romans do it in legion.
Ronald Reagan does it to your tired, your poor.
Roofers do it on the roof.*
Room clerks do it with reservation.
Roosters do it cockily.*
Rope makers do it cordially.
Rosalynn Carter does it for peanuts.
Royal Canadians do it mountingly.*
Rubik does it solidly but twistedly.
Rudolph does it with his red protuberance.*
Rugby players do it with leather balls.
Rulers do it inch by inch.
Rulers do it measuredly.*
Rumple did it and skinned his stilt.
Russell and Whitehead did it symbolically.
Russians do it redily.

S

Sadists do it smartly.*
Sages do it spicily.
Sages do it wisely.
Sailors do it buoyantly.
Sailors do it by getting blown at sea.
Sailors do it nautilly.
Sailors do it sheepishly.*
Sailors do it tackily.
Sailors do it with seamen.
Salesmen do it on the road.
San Franciscans do it, but it's a drag.

San Franciscans do it shakily.*
Sancho Panza did it on his ass.
Sandhogs do it from underneath.
Sandra Day O'Connor does it on a bench
with eight old men.
Sartre did it existentially.
Satan does it temptingly.
Satirists do it bitingly.
Saul does it with a bellow.*
Sausage makers do it the wurst way.
Savages do it wildly.*
Schizophrenics do it twice.*
Scholars do it marginally.
Scholars do it for grants.
Schopenhauer did it pessimistically.
Schubert did it incompletely.
Schubert did it without finishing it.*
Schubert did it with four trouts.*
Science teachers do it with test tubes.
Scientists do it experimentally.
Scottish musicians do it by squeezing their bags.*
Scrimpy diners do it with poor tips.
Scuba divers do it tanked.
Sculptors do it until it's hard.
Sculptors do it with hard rocks.
Sea birds do it in gullies.
Seals do it with their balls.
Seamstresses do it sew-sew.
Secretaries do it 8 to 5.
Secretaries do it in triplicate.
Secretaries do it shorthandedly.
Semanticists do it word for word.
Semioticians do it symbolically.*
Senior citizens do it in their dreams.
Senior citizens do it retiringly.

Señoritas do it by rolling their *r*'s.
Sentries do it haltingly.
Sentries do it guardedly.
Septuagenarians do it weakly weekly.*
Serial librarians do it periodically.*
Service station attendants do it with Ethyl.
Set designers do it obscenely.
Seven-Up freaks undo it.
Shad do it roefully.
Shakespeare did it playfully.
Shakespeare did it tempestuously.
Shakespeare did it willingly.*
Shakespeare did it willy-nilly.*
Shamans do it bewitchingly.
Sharp people do it keenly.
Sharpshooters do it with their pistols cocked.
Sheepherders do it on the lam.
Sheep do it when they want to kid.
Shelley did it to a skylark.
Shepherds do it with their rod.
Sherlock Holmes did it elementary.
Sherlock Holmes did it with Watson.*
Shoe salesmen do it solefully.
Shoemakers give it their awl.
Shoeshines do it in the buff.
Short-order cooks do it sunnyside up.
Shriners do it conventionally.*
Shriners do it voluntarily.
Siamese twins do it together.
Simon did it simply.
Simpletons do it easily.
Sinatra does it frankly.
Singers do it with their tongue.*
Sinking sailors do it balefully.
Sir Thomas did it More.
Sirens do it alarmingly.

Sirens do it screamingly.*
Skeptics do it incredulously.*
Skiers do it in the snow.
Skiers do it on the slope.
Skunks do it distinctly.
Skunks do it for a cent.
Slavs do it with poles.
Smart asses do it with wise cracks.
Smokers blow it.*
Smokers do it with their butt.
Snails do it slowly.*
Snake charmers do it venomously.
Sneaks do it without telling anybody.
Sneaky *a tergo* lovers do it behind your back.*
Snow White did it happily, sleepily,
grumpily, sneezingly, bashfully, dopily,
and then she got docked.
Snow White did it seven times.
Snow White did it with the dwarfs.
Soccer players do it for kicks.
Soccer players do it for ninety minutes.
Soccer players do it with eleven men.
Soccer players do it with leather balls.
Sociologists do it with large groups of people.
Socrates did it questioningly.
Sodomites do it fruitfully.*
Sodomites do it with rectitude.
Soldiers do it in private.*
Soldiers do it patriotically.*
Soldiers do it privately.
Soldiers do it uniformly.*
Soothsayers do it auspiciously.
Sopranos do it broadly.
Sopranos do it on key.
Sopranos do it on the high seas.

South Africans do it boeringly.
South Africans do it randily.
Southern belles peel to do it.
Spa guests do it in hot water.
Space travelers do it on Uranus.*
Spaniards do it mainly in the plain.
Speakers do it chairfully.
Speech teachers do it orally.*
Speed skaters do it on ice.
Spelunkers do it in caves.*
Spenser did it in the fairie queene.
Sphinxes do it enigmatically.
Spies do it secretly.
Spies do it under cover.*
Spinoza did it ethically.
Spiritualists do it with no body.
Squirrels do it with their nuts.*
Standup comedians do it for laughs.
Statisticians do it averagely.*
Statisticians do it with mean deviates.*
Steam fitters do it under pressure.
Steel workers do it with red-hot rods.
Steeplechasers do it overridingly.
Stephen Sondheim does it melodically.*
Stevie does it wonderfully.
Stockbrokers do it marginally.
Stockbrokers do it over the counter.
Stockbrokers do it prospectively.
Stockholders do it by proxy.
Story tellers do it with their tale.
Stradivarius fiddled around doing it.*
Stravinsky did it right in spring.*
Streakers do it in the flesh.
Strikers do it protestingly.
Strippers do it barely.

Strippers do it teasingly.
Structured programmers do it to perform and release.
Studs do it polysemously.*
Stuntmen do it head-over-heels.
Stutterers d... d... d... do it.
Stutterers do it hesitatingly.
Stutterers do it repeatedly.
Subscribers do it with checks.
Suit salesmen do it in brooks.
Sunburned people do it readily.
Sunworshippers do it tantalizingly.
Superman does it faster than a speedy bull.*
Surfers do it on a board.
Surfers do it waveringly.
Surgeons do it cuttingly.
Surgeons do it incisively.
Surgeons do it internally.
Surgeons do it with retractors.
Surgery patients are in stitches doing it.
Surveyors do it horizontally.
Surveyors do it on the level.
Swedes do it socially.
Swimmers get wet doing it.
Swimmers do it with breaststrokes.*
Swimmers do it with the right strokes.
Swiss cheese makers do it with
a holier-than-thou attitude.
Swordsmen do it thrustingly.*
Swordsmen do it to the hilt.
Sycophants do it praisingly.*
Systems analysts do it with black box models.

T

T.S. Eliot did it with a bang, followed by a whimper.*
Teaching assistants do it with class.
Taffy makers pull it.
Tailors seam to do it.
Tailors do it fitfully.
Tailors do it fittingly.
Tailors do it pantingly.
Tailors do it with anyone suitable.
Tailors do it unalterably.
Tailors keep you in stitches when they do it.
Tank drivers do it tirelessly.
Tantalus did it tantalizingly.*
Taste-testers do it by eating it.
Tautologists do it repeatedly again several times.*
Tax collectors do it quarterly.*
Taxi drivers do it for tips.
Taxi drivers do it with their meters running.
Taxi drivers do it fairly.
Taxidermists do it stuffily.
Taxidermists stuff it.*
Tchaikovsky did it with a nutcracker.*
Tea merchants do it with bags.
Teachers make you do it until you do it right.
Teachers do it with class.
Teamsters do it with dollies.
Tearoom readers do it in the leaves.
Teddy Roosevelt did it with a big stick.
Telephone operators do it by the numbers.
Telephone operators do it with hang-ups.
Tennis players do it by taking their balls out of cans.
Tennis players make a racquet when they do it.
Tennis players do it backhandedly.
Tennis players do it for love.

Tennis players jump over the net after they did it.*
Terminal repairmen do it after
removing their lockstraps.
Terns do it good.
Terrorists do it explosively.
Testators do it willingly.
Texans do it with their long horns.*
The Devil made me do it.
The Incredible Hulk does it until he turns green.
The IRS does it by tightening your loopholes.
The Marquis de Sade did it painfully.
The Marquis did it sadistically.
The Moral Majority does it religiously.
The Wright Brothers did it over Kitty Hawk.
Theoreticians do it, theoretically speaking.
Theo did it baldly.
Theologians do it divinely.
Therapists do it for 50 minutes.
Thermodynamicists do it with black bodies.
Thieves do it stealthily.*
Thomas Aquinas did it summarily.
Thomas did it crappily.
Ticket agents do it reservedly.
Timekeepers do it around the clock.
Timers do it in hundreths of a second.
Tinkerbell did it with Pan's peter.
Title searchers do it abstractly.
Toads do it hornily.
Tom did it dooly.
Tom did it pipingly.
Tom did it swiftly.
Tom does it with Dick and Harry.*
Tomcats do it with little pussies.
Top models do it beautifully.
Tracy did it with his dick.*

Traditional brides do it in June.
Traffic police do it pointedly.
Trailblazers do it in virgin territory.
Train conductors do it in a timely manner.
Trainers do it with demonstrations.
Transsexuals do it ambiguously.
Transvestites do it one way or another.
Travel agents do it on airplanes, busses and ships.*
Tree surgeons do it out on a limb.
Tree trimmers go out on a limb to do it.
Tree fellers do it and leave.
Triplets do it thrice.*
Tristan did it knightly with Isolde through a philter.
Troglodytes did it in caves.*
Trombonists do it on a slide.
Trouser makers do it pantingly.
Truckers shift gears while doing it.
Truckers do it with big rigs.
Truman Capote did it in cold blood.*
Trumpeters do it hornily.*
Tuba players do it way down low.
Turtle soup makers do it mockingly.
TV actors do it commercially.
Twins double your fun doing it.*
Twins do it identically.
Twins do it two.
Typists do it by touch.
Typists do it hunt and peck.
Typists do it marginally.
Typists do it on key.
Typists do it with their fingers.

U

Ultra-feminists do it hersterically.*
Umpires do it arbitrarily.
Uncle Mal does it (a)maniacally.*
Uncle Mal does it once a year.
Undertakers do it gravely.*
Undertakers do it rigorously mortified.
Undertakers do it with any body.
Unicorns do it fabulously with their horn.
Union members do it collectively.
Union officials do it strikingly.
University graduate professors do it unfailingly.
Untrained joggers do it stiffly.
Upholsterers do it tacky.*
Upright citizens do it on pillars.
Urolagnia freaks do it with golden showers.*
Urologists do it in puddles.*
Urologists do it pithily.
Used car salesmen do it tirelessly.
Ushers do it in the aisles.

V

Valley girls do it for sure.*
Vampires do it cryptically.
Van Gogh did it earily.
Vatican altar boys did it imPiously.*
Vegetarians do it with carrots and cucumbers.
Venetians do it blindly.
Venetians do it in their canals.
Ventriloquists do it unmovingly.
Ventriloquists do it with dummies.
Ventriloquists do it without moving their lips.

Venus de Milo did it without her arms.*
Vermonters do it syruptitiously.
Veterinarians do it bestially.
Veterinarians do it doggedly.
Veterinarians do it with animals.
Viennese do it waltzingly.
Vietnamese do it advisedly.
Vikings did it hornily.
Villa-Lobos did it chorosively.
Vintners do it in the cellar.
Vintners do it whiningly.
Violinists do it gutsily.
Violinists do it unstrungly.*
Violinists do it while fiddling around.
Violinists do it with strings attached.
Violinists do it with their F-holes.
Virgin Mary didn't do it.
Virginalists do it with their fingers.
Virgins do it intactly.
Voyeurs do it from peek to peek.
Vulcanologists do it eruptingly.

W

Wage negotiators do it retroactively.
Wagnalls does it funkily.*
Wagner did it heroically.
Wagner did it with a flying Dutchman.*
Wagnerians do it for days straight.
Waiters do it with their tips.
Walruses do it with tusks.
Wardens do it with conviction.
Washingtonians do it diplomatically.*
WASPs do it stingily.

Watchmakers do it in their own good time.
Watchmakers do it with jeweled movements.
Watchmen do it by the hour.
Weathermen do it frontally.
Weathermen do it in vane.
Weathermen do it low and in front.
Weathermen do it under high pressure.
Weathermen do it with different systems.
Weavers do it until they dye.
Weavers do it with a twist.
Webster did it word for word.
Weightlifters do it with straining.
Weightwatchers do it through thick and thin.
Weightwatchers get applause for not doing it.
Welders do it with a hot torch.
Welfare recipients do it dolefully.
Welfare recipients do it poorly.
Welsh do it with rabbits.*
White-collar workers do it professionally.
Who done it?*
Whores do it trickily.*
Widows do it lamentingly.*
Widows do it merrily.*
Wigmakers do it with hairpieces.
Wild bears do it grisly.
Will did it with his spear, shakily.*
William F. Buckley, Jr. does it with his *plumbum* and
extraordinarily facile lingual contortions.*
William James did it pragmatically.
William did it conqueringly.
William did it tellingly.
Wind surfers do it standing up.
Winemakers do it with aplomb.
Wise people anticipate doing it.
Witch doctors do it charmingly.*

Witches do it magically.
Witches do it with brooms.
Wolves do it howlingly.
Wordsworth did it throughout a very long excursion.
Wreckers do it with big iron balls.
Writers do it with their pen.
Writers do it literally.*
Writers do it when they aren't blocked.
Writers do it with Flair.

X

X-ray technicians do it in all positions.
X-ray technicians do it transparently.
X-ray technicians do it with penetration.
Xerox salesmen do it for reproduction.

Y

Yachtsmen do it tackily.
Yankees do it doodly.
Yell leaders do it cheerfully.
Yeti do it with their bigfeet.
Yogis do it with their legs crossed.
Young men's club members do it Yly.
Young women do it grippingly.*

Z

Zeus did it with a swan.*
Zookeepers do it with animals.
Zorba did it the Greek way.*